Núria & Empar Jiménez
Rosa M. Curto

Taking care of your planet

Splash!

water

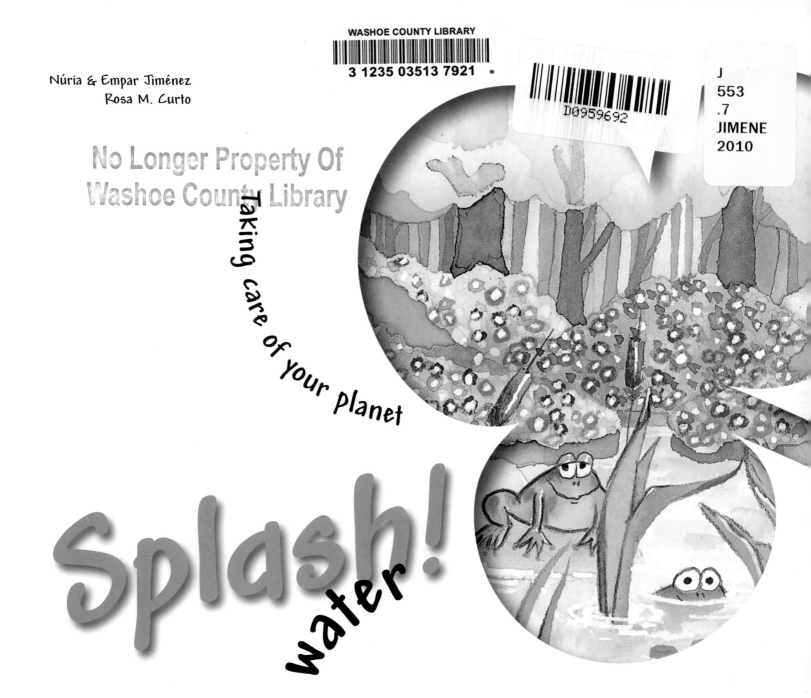

BARRON'S

Have you been playing in the street? It's very hot, and you're very hot and very, very thirsty. You need water! You go running to the sink. You fill up a large glass of water and . . . yum! It's nice and cool! How lovely! Can you imagine if not even a trickle of water came out of the faucet? Where is the nearest spring?

Some villages don't have sinks with faucets, or springs. They don't even have water. The people who live there have to go a very long way to collect water from wells, and it isn't always good to drink.

Do you like jumping in puddles and playing with mud? You probably wind up covered in mud from head to toe. But you can get cleaned up with a good shower. If we didn't have water, we would be very dirty. And what about your clothes, the plates you eat from, and the floor of your house? You always need water for washing, don't you?

Water is used for watering the plants on the balcony and the vegetables and trees in the garden. You also use it when you play or swim at the beach or in a river or lake or pool. What fun it is jumping over the waves!

Our planet has a lot of
water. It has so much that the
planet appears blue when seen
from space. Imagine if we could place all the water on
Earth in an enormous pitcher full to the top. If you could pour
one hundred glasses of water from that pitcher, only one glass
would be freshwater. The rest of the glasses would be the saltwater
of the seas and oceans.

Almost all the freshwater is found underground, and a large amount of
the water found at the surface is in the form of ice. So, if you could pour
another one hundred glasses of water from that glass of freshwater, only
one glass would be the water found in rivers, lakes, and clouds.
That's not very much, is it?

As you can see, water is a treasure. It takes a lot of effort to obtain it, but it gets dirty quickly. If we throw garbage into it, it becomes polluted immediately and can ruin the environment. We have to be very careful.

Even when we don't do anything bad, every time we use water, we dirty it and it cannot be reused. Can you imagine if you had to drink water from the drains? Ugh! How disgusting!

The dirty water from the villages and cities ends up in water treatment plants, where it is treated and cleaned. More than half the water that reaches the water treatment plants is returned to the rivers and the sea a little bit cleaner. Despite the treatment, this water is not clean enough; it's not clean enough to drink again. This water can be used only to water the fields, to clean the streets, and for industry.

Fortunately, there are many things you can do
to save water in your home, and they are all very simple!

When you brush your teeth or wash your hands,
turn off the faucet while you brush and soap.
Then you'll be able to save a whole pitcherful of water.
Did you know that when you take a bath you might use
as much water as if you took two to four four-minute
showers?

You can save a lot of water with the washing machine and dishwasher if you turn them on only when they are completely full. You can also save water if you flush the toilet only when it's necessary.

If you must water the plants, it's best to do so early in the morning or in the evening, to prevent the water from evaporating. Have you ever thought of watering the plants with the water you used to wash vegetables, or with rainwater?

Did you know that half of your body is water? If you could melt like an ice block, you would almost fill up a whole bucket! Water is very important for the body. We all need to drink water every day. And when it's very hot, we need to drink more water, eat fruit, and consume other refreshing food and drink to avoid getting dehydrated. We may also need to apply lotion to moisturize our skin.

Water is mischievous and it likes to play. Sometimes it goes up and down, or jumps like a waterfall. It can be very, very hot, like soup; or it can be very cold, like ice.

It amuses itself to dress up and change shape. It can hide in the air so that you can't see it. It can be liquid and runny. Try holding it in your hand and you will see how it runs away! Sometimes, it is as hard as a rock or as soft as fresh snow.

Traveling is one of the things it likes doing the most.

Do you know where water comes from? And where it goes to?
Water falls from the sky in the form of rain, hail, or snow.
Some of this water escapes to underground streams.
Then it reaches the rivers, lakes, and the sea.

When it is very hot, you become covered with drops of sweat,
which comes from the water in your body. If you were a lake,
your sweat droplets would rise upward and upward to the sky
to become clouds. And when the clouds released the water
droplets in the form of rain, the cycle would start over again.

Water is a great traveler, and it always follows the same route.

Sometimes, however, the gentle cycle is disrupted and it can rain a lot over a short period of time. Then the water might not be absorbed by the soil, and it accumulates to cause flooding. Sometimes, the rain falls in the form of hailstones. If this happens, you should look for shelter. Hail can hurt, and it can cause injury!

If the wind and rains are very strong, the sea seems to get angry, causing the waves to grow and grow and sweep away everything they find in their path. You must be very careful!

As you can see, water is very, very important. We couldn't live without it, could we? That's why we all need to make some effort not to spoil it. We must all try to do our part, so that one day we will be able to see our rivers, lakes, and seas nice and clean and full of life.

I do my part. What about you? You can help, too!

Activities

The dripping faucet

Have you ever thought about how much water is lost every day from a faucet that is not turned off properly? Experiment: Place a glass underneath the faucet. Turn the faucet on, just enough to let it drip. Wait five minutes and observe how much water there is in the glass. Imagine how much would be lost in a day! By the way, remember to turn the faucet off when you've finished experimenting!

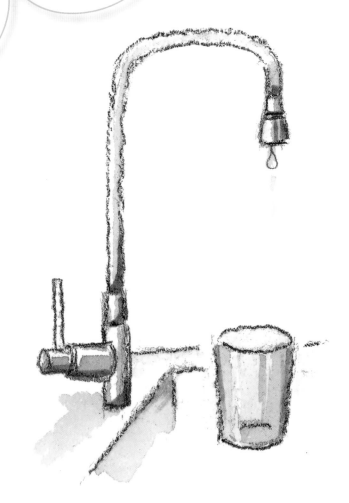

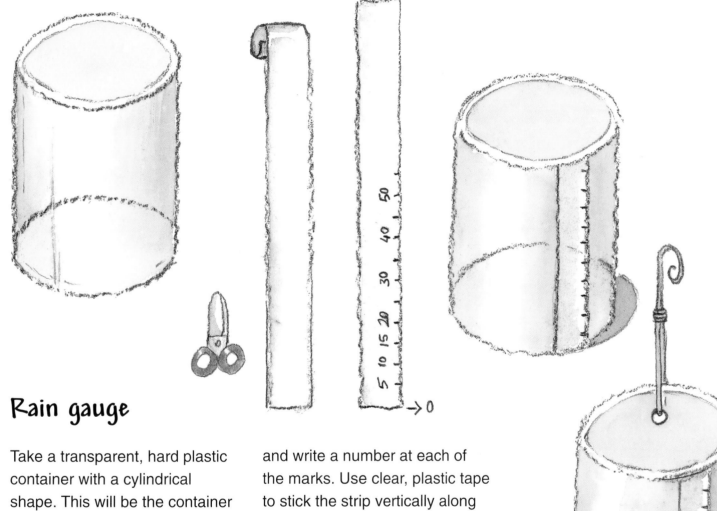

Rain gauge

Take a transparent, hard plastic container with a cylindrical shape. This will be the container for your rain gauge. Very carefully cut out a strip of tracing paper two or three fingers wide. Mark the paper every millimeter, starting with 0 at the bottom. If you find this too difficult, you can make marks every 5 millimeters, and write a number at each of the marks. Use clear, plastic tape to stick the strip vertically along the container so that the 0 is at the bottom. Ask an adult to help you make a hook from a piece of wire to hang the rain gauge outside, so that you can record how much rain falls every day at home or at school.

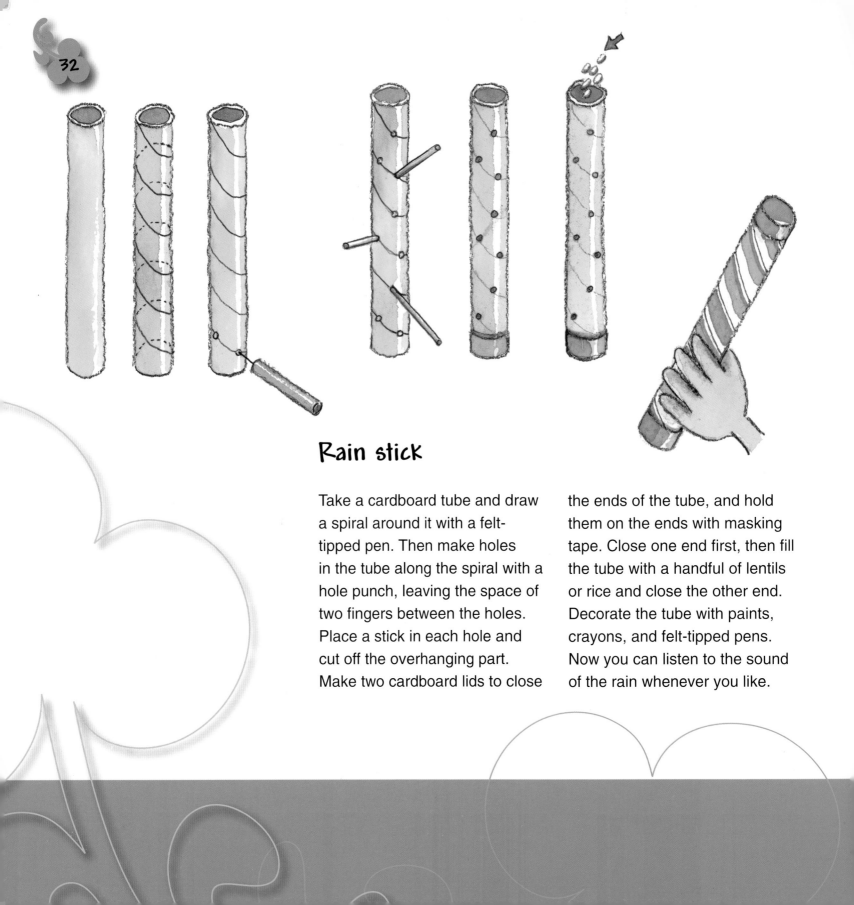

Rain stick

Take a cardboard tube and draw a spiral around it with a felt-tipped pen. Then make holes in the tube along the spiral with a hole punch, leaving the space of two fingers between the holes. Place a stick in each hole and cut off the overhanging part. Make two cardboard lids to close the ends of the tube, and hold them on the ends with masking tape. Close one end first, then fill the tube with a handful of lentils or rice and close the other end. Decorate the tube with paints, crayons, and felt-tipped pens. Now you can listen to the sound of the rain whenever you like.

The water cycle

Pour some water into a clear plastic bag. Blow it up and tie it up with a rubber band so that the water and air cannot escape. Place the bag on a sunny windowsill. After a while, you will see how the bag begins to sweat and the sides are covered with tiny droplets of water.

Parents' guide

Where is the nearest spring? (pages 2–3)
You can explain to children how difficult it is to access drinking water in other parts of the planet. Although people may have water, such as in Bangladesh or in India, this does not mean that it is of good quality. Furthermore, people don't always have the necessary resources to purify the water. Children need to understand that dirty water can cause illnesses and that's why it is important to have clean water for drinking.

The water on the planet (pages 6–7)
This section can be worked on with the help of a map or globe. Water covers 70 percent of our planet's surface, but almost all of it is found in the seas and oceans. You can explain that water is found in the form of ice at the poles. At the North Pole, there is just water beneath the ice. Hence, the North Pole is only accessible when the Arctic Ocean is frozen. On the other hand, in the south, in Antarctica, there is land beneath the ice. If the ice melted, the sea level would rise. Also, ice can always be found on the highest mountains, such as the Himalayas and the Andes, as well as in glaciers. You can also mention that in some parts of the planet, such as in the tropics, it rains a lot, and in other places, such as in the desert zones of Africa, it hardly ever rains. This

ensures that water is very poorly shared. This explanation can be related to the water cycle.

Purifying water (pages 10–11)
You can explain to children that water treatment plants are like factories for cleaning the water. They are more efficient, however, if the water that enters them is relatively clean. If the sewer water contains oils, fats, and solvents, for example, it can prevent the plant from functioning properly, and the water leaving it will not be as clean as it should be. Children should understand that the water that comes out of these plants cannot be drunk, and the plants responsible for producing drinking water are water purification plants. The water entering water purification plants must be quite clean. Depending on the children's age, you could also introduce the topic of energy consumption: Like other factories, purification plants need energy to pump the water, to oxygenize it, and so on.

Let's save water (pages 12–15)
Children feel useful and important when you involve them in domestic tasks, according to their age. Saving water can be considered a task for the whole family. For example, you can

encourage the children to take care of the houseplants, and water them in the evening and in the morning before going to school. They can also help to fill up the dishwasher and the washing machine. And you can teach them that the toilet is not a garbage can and that it should only be flushed when necessary. It is essential to acknowledge the children's involvement in these tasks with positive comments and praise, which will encourage them to continue with their good work.

Water is the source of life (pages 18–19)

It is very important that children understand that water is essential not only for humans but also for all living things. You could make a list of living things that need water to survive and say what they need it for. You can speak about animals and plants that live in water and also those that use it to look for food or to reproduce (like palm trees that need water to disperse their coconuts) or simply for drinking and bathing. The list will surely grow! If the children show an interest, you can introduce the concept of food chains.

Properties of water (pages 22–23)

In this section, you can introduce children to the properties of water, which have specific characteristics. You can fill up a glass with water and observe it. Children can easily start to point out the first characteristics: It is transparent, it doesn't smell, and it has no taste. You can also use an ice cube to observe other properties—for example, that water is the only substance on Earth that can naturally be found as a solid (ice), a liquid, and a gas (water vapor), and that the ice floats on liquid water.

Depending on the children's interest and age, you can also explain to them that water can take a while to heat up, but once it is warm, it maintains its temperature for quite a long time, which is why it is used in heating and cooling devices. Also, for this reason, winters are not so cold in areas near the coast. In the form of ice, water is an excellent insulator. The temperature inside an igloo can be 72°F (40 C°) higher than on the outside.

In a simple manner, children can also discover other properties: Water has a great capacity for dissolving substances. You can test this with salt, sugar, or coffee and observe what happens. However, it cannot be mixed with certain other substances, like oil.

The water cycle and angry water (pages 24–27)

The water cycle can be explained very briefly. To tie this in with the previous chapter, you can say that the right conditions are found on Earth for water to be found in three different states. When it is hot, water tends to evaporate. In the clouds, the water vapor cools and condenses. If it is very, very cold, the water solidifies and forms snow and ice. If the temperature warms a little, it becomes liquid again and falls in the form of rain, or it is liquid first and then it solidifies and falls in the form of hailstones.

Depending on the age of the children, you can say that while rainwater is good for harvests and for cleaning the environment, great snowfalls and hailstorms can cause damage. Similarly, you can talk to them about different phenomena that occur in coastal zones due to the effects of water (flooding, sharp increases in sea level, and so on). You should explain this in such a way that the children see it as a natural process and are not too alarmed by it.

Splash! water

Original title of the book in Catalan:
Cuidem el Planeta: Xof! L'aigua
© Copyright Gemser Publications S.L., 2010.
C/ Castell, 38; Teià (08329) Barcelona, Spain (World Rights)
Tel: 93 540 13 53
E-mail: info@mercedesros.com
Website: www.mercedesros.com
Authors: Núria & Empar Jiménez
Illustrator: Rosa María Curto

First edition for the United States and Canada published
2010 by Barron's Educational Series, Inc.

All inquiries should be addressed to:
Barron's Educational Series, Inc.
250 Wireless Boulevard
Hauppauge, New York 11788
www.barronseduc.com

ISBN-13: 978-0-7641-4544-5
ISBN-10: 0-7641-4544-4

Library of Congress Control No.: 2009943888

Manufactured by: L. Rex Printing Co. LTD.,
Tin Wan, China
Date of Manufacture: August 2010

Printed in China
9 8 7 6 5 4 3 2 1